Northern Bee Books
Scout Bottom Farm
Mytholmroyd
Hebden Bridge
HX7 5JS (UK)

www.northernbeebooks.co.uk
Tel: 01422 882751

© 2018

ISBN: 978-1-912271-30-6

Printed by Lightning Source, UK

Making Beeswax Flowers

by Elizabeth Duffin

Preface

Michael and I have kept bees for forty years and it was in the early days that I first saw beeswax flowers at the Royal Bath & West of England Show. As we were considering entering a big display, I was keen to find out how to make wax flowers to decorate it. Not many people were making them then and there was very little by way of instructions at that time. But, I was determined to have a go and my first effort was a water lily and lily pad, which I have included in this book. From there, I went on to make various flowers for our display and, also for the wax flower classes at the Bath and West and the National Honey Show. So that is how it all started and I hope you enjoy what I have put in this book.

My thanks also to Michael for taking all the pictures.

Elizabeth Duffin

Materials for the flowers

Clean Beeswax

Stub Wires from the florists for stems and leaves

Candle Dyes

Florist Binding Tape

Cotton Wool

Cotton threads for stamens

Thin covered wire (as used for sugar paste flowers)

Mains cable plastic covered wire for larger flowers

Other things you will need or find useful: -

A piece of exterior plywood approx. 190mm x 130mm

A plain smooth silicone mat

A small ladle such as a measuring spoon

Spoons of various sizes and shapes

A large bowl of cold water

A small bowl of cold water with washing up liquid added

Scissors and/or a craft knife

A sheet of glass approx. 200mm x 200mm with ground edges (or sharp edges taped for safety)

A bowl for melting the wax and a pan to hold the bowl.

An electric ring or hob

Knitting needles for stirring the wax.

Making flat sheets of wax for petals and leaves

Use clean filtered wax – N.B. do not overheat the wax as it will darken and become more brittle. Always use a water bath to melt the wax, never on direct heat.

Soak the piece of plywood in cold water, the moisture will stop the wax from sticking. If you are using a silicone sheet, it will need clipping to a sheet of stiff plastic such as corex board. This will not need wetting as the wax will not adhere.

Heat the wax in the bowl over hot water (remember to top up the water as needed).

For green wax add a small amount of green dye and stir to melt. **(Pictures 1,2 & 3).**

Pour a test sheet to check for colour and add more dye if required. As you are using yellow wax, allow for this when mixing, adding small amounts of blue to get a good colour. The dyes can be mixed in the same way as paints adding colours as required.

When the wax is completely melted, pour the wax in a ladle down the wet board **(Picture 4)** or silicone sheet, **(Picture 5)** collecting the run-off in the bowl. (Make sure that your board is no wider than the bowl). Then ladle cold water down the board **(Picture 6)** into the coldwater bowl and peel off the sheet of wax. If a thicker sheet is required, pour more wax over the board when the first sheet has set before dipping it in the water. A longer sheet will need a longer board and a larger ladle. If the colour of the sheet is not as you want it, add more dye to the bowl, putting the wrong colour sheet back in the bowl to melt. As the wax in the bowl is over water and has a large surface area, overheating should not be a problem. Dry the sheets on kitchen roll or a clean cloth, they will have a smooth and a rough side. You are now ready to cut petals and leaves.

3

4

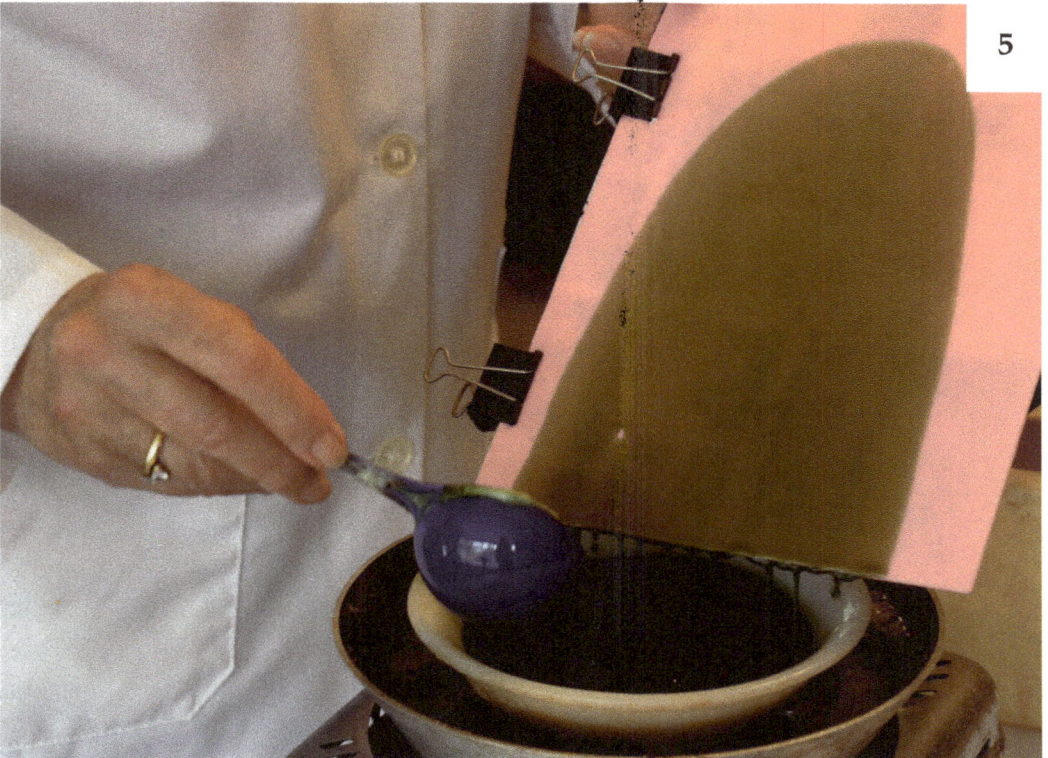

5

6

This photograph shows the use of flat sheets of wax for petals and leaves on a Fuchsia.

Making roses

For a small rose use the patterns shown, making card patterns from the diagrams. For the small rose you will need – 1 circle, 1 small petal, 1 small calyx, 1 top leaf and 1 side leaf.

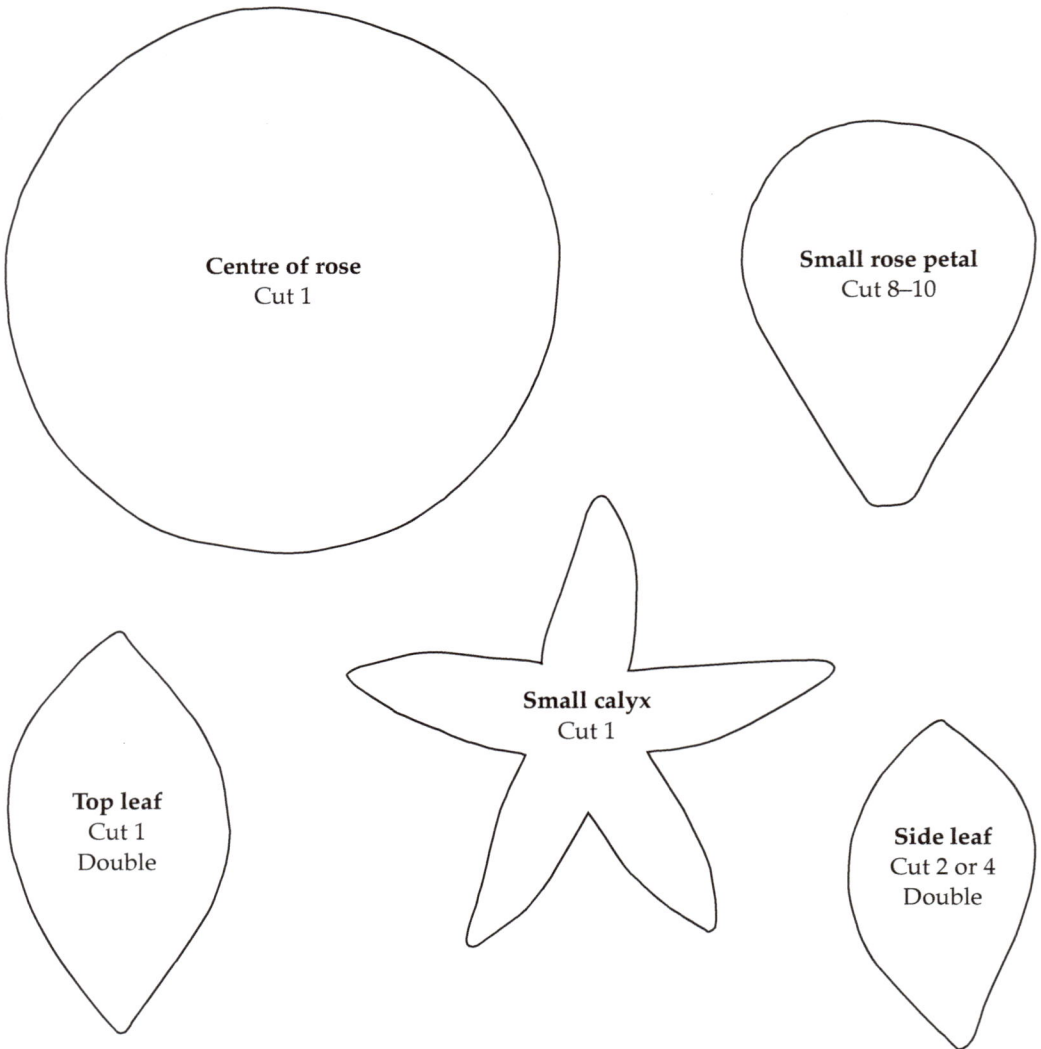

Centre of rose
Cut 1

Small rose petal
Cut 8–10

Small calyx
Cut 1

Top leaf
Cut 1
Double

Side leaf
Cut 2 or 4
Double

**Small water
lily petal**
Cut 8

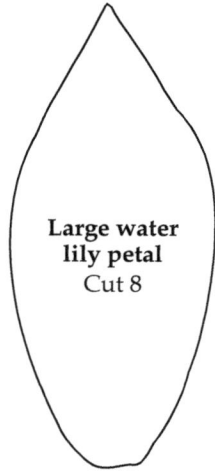

**Large water
lily petal**
Cut 8

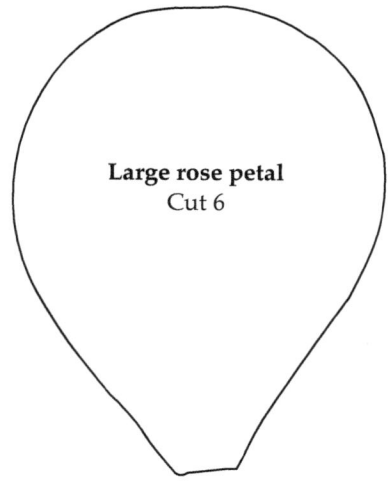

Large rose petal
Cut 6

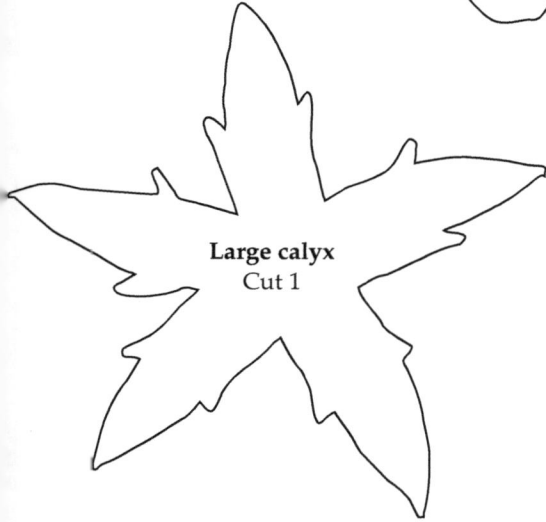

Large calyx
Cut 1

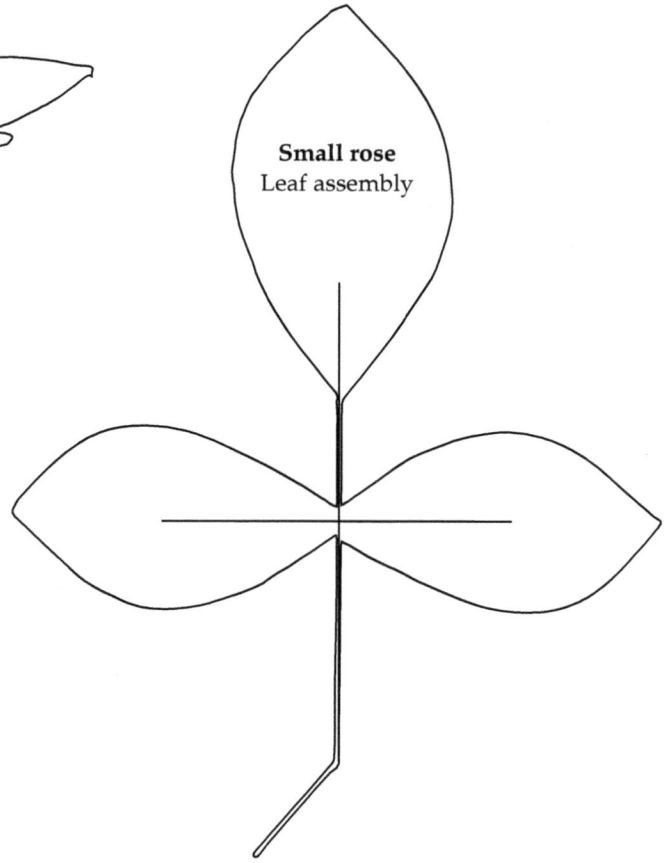

Small rose
Leaf assembly

Crocus leaf
Cut 5

From the colour you have chosen for the rose, cut 8 – 10 small petals and one circle for the centre together with one green calyx.

Place a sheet of the coloured wax onto the glass and use the craft knife to cut around the petal pattern. As this is a simple shape, you may prefer to use scissors.

Twist a wisp of cotton wool round the top of an 80mm stub wire, then fold the top part of the wire over to stop the cotton wool unrolling. Bind the wire with florists' tape, starting from the bottom of the cotton wool, down the length of the wire, pulling it firmly at an angle. Dip the cotton wool into melted beeswax, this will give a base to attach the petals. Push the bottom of the wire through the circle, smooth side down and push it up to the waxed cotton wool. Then fold in half and press along the fold and onto the wax blob, leaving the curved edges loose. Fold in half again and press the two folded edges together, again leaving the curves loose. Roll over, keeping the top to a point and squash the wax at the bottom onto the wire. You will now have the appearance of four petals unfurling.

Now shape the first petal. Rub the edges to smooth them and to warm the wax between your fingers. Next, press your thumb into the centre of the petal, supported on two fingers. You can then roll the upper edges to give you a reflexed petal. (Picture 7).

7

You are now ready to attach this petal to the centre. Keeping the top of the petal close to the top of the centre, fold it round, pressing the excess wax onto the wire. (Picture 8) Continue shaping and adding petals, overlapping each one halfway over the previous one, until you are happy with the shape making sure you pull the excess wax down the stem with your fingers. (Picture 9)

Now add the calyx. Push the stem wire through the centre of the calyx, smooth side up and ease it up to the base of the petals with your fingers. (Picture 10) Cut off some of the excess wax on the stem and then, with a scrap of green wax, wind it round the coloured wax up to the calyx and shape it with your fingers to form a rose hip. (Picture 11) You are now ready to make the leaves.

The leaves are double, so put two sheets of green wax together, rough sides together. Cut out one top leaf and two side leaves. (Picture 12) Cut a 40mm length of stub wire and wrap it tightly with the florists' tape. (Picture 13) Sandwich the top leaf over the top 12mm of

13

11

14

12

15

the wire and press firmly together. Wind a 42mm length of very thin wire round the stem, 15mm below the top leaf (I prefer the type of wire with a paper coating, available from sugar paste suppliers, but you could use 5amp fuse wire), leaving 15mm protruding at both ends. (Picture 14) Now add the two small leaves, sandwiched round the protruding wire, overlapping them in the centre. (Picture 15) To make them more stable, paint molten green wax on both sides at the base of the top leaf and on both sides of the join of the two side leaves.

16

17

18

Now lay the leaves on a sheet of glass and mark veins on each of the leaves (an empty ball point pen is suitable for this). (Picture 16) Look at a real rose if you can, to see how they go. Rose leaves have serrated edges, and this can be done by cutting into the edge of the leaf and twisting the scissors. (Picture 17) Repeat all the way round. Bend the wire 22mm from the bottom at an angle. Wrap more tape on the wire, starting at the rose hip, covering it completely. Wrap the tape down about 1/3rd of the stem wire, hold the bent piece of the wire against the stem and continue wrapping the tape to hold the leaf in place, (Picture 18) and continue to the bottom of the stem. Your first flower is now complete. (Picture 19)

19

For a large rose you will need a thicker stem, plastic coated mains wire about 420mm long is suitable. Remove about 20mm of the plastic coating and then continue as for the small rose. Form the centre, then add 8 – 10 small petals. You will need to cut 6 large petals and these should be added as before. Cut a large green calyx and push it up to the petals. Make a rose hip as for the small rose. Make a leaf with one top leaf and one pair as before. This is the first leaf 70mm below the flower, the next one has one top leaf and two pairs of side leaves and needs a longer central wire, 110mm approx. but is made and attached in the same way. (Picture 20)

A number of flowers can be made using flat sheets of wax, but very cupped shaped petals can be made using spoons dipped in wax. I will show you how to use this method.

Making a Crocus

You will need to find a spoon with a bowl as near as the petal shape as possible (Picture 21).

For the crocus, I am using the right hand spoon. (Charity shops can be a useful source of odd spoons). Have a bowl of cold water with some yellow washing up liquid added. This is to break the surface tension of the water, so it will coat the spoon evenly. Dip the spoon into the water, push it into purple molten wax, then tip it so that the bowl end of the spoon comes out first. (Picture 22) Drain the liquid wax off one side of the bowl of the spoon next to the handle. Repeat, draining the wax off the other side. (Picture 23) Now cut around the edge of the spoon with a knife. (Picture 24) Put the bowl of the spoon into the palm of your other hand and ease the spoon off sideways, leaving the petal in your hand. (Picture 25) Then with your thumb, ease the petal off the bowl of the spoon sideways and discard back into the melted wax. (Picture 26) The petal from the back of the spoon is the one to use. Repeat until you have 6 petals per flower.

21

22

23

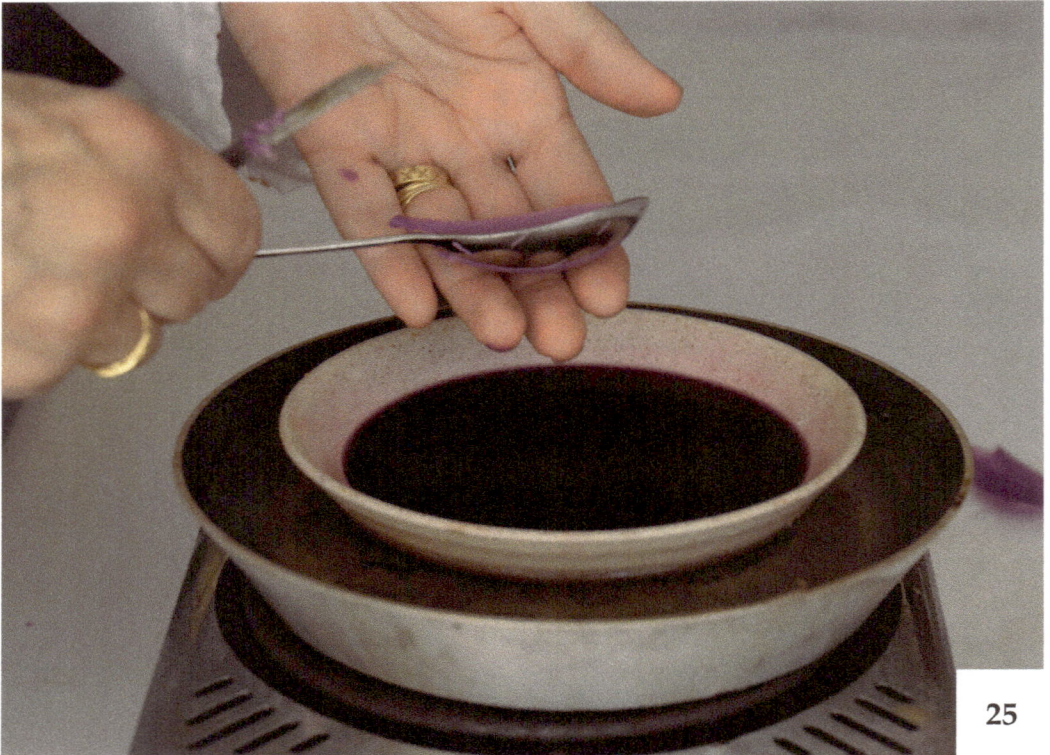

26

27

28

29

The stems are made the same way as for the rose, using a 90mm length of stub wire. You will also need 5 stamens for the centre of the flower. These are made by dipping lengths of cotton thread into orange molten wax. (Pictures 27 & 28) You must use cotton thread, as the wax will not be absorbed by manmade fibres. Cut five pieces about 40mm long and dip the end of one of them into the molten wax to build up a "pollen" blob (Picture 29). Press the one with the pollen blob onto the wax on the wire stem and press the other four round it. Roll a narrow scrap of green wax round the base of the stamens to give you a base to attach the petals. Carefully rub the edges of the petals to make them smooth. Attach three petals round the stem (see picture) pressing them firmly at the base. Attach the remaining three petals over the previous ones, with the centre overlapping the edges of the first row. (Picture 30)

30

Now make 5 leaves (see pattern). Cut out the leaves and press a length of white thread down the centre. Turn the tip of the leaf over the top of the thread to secure it. Use a scrap of green wax at the base of the thread to hold it in place. (Picture 31) Press the leaves onto the stem evenly round the flower, so that the tips of the leaves are about level with the tops of the petals.

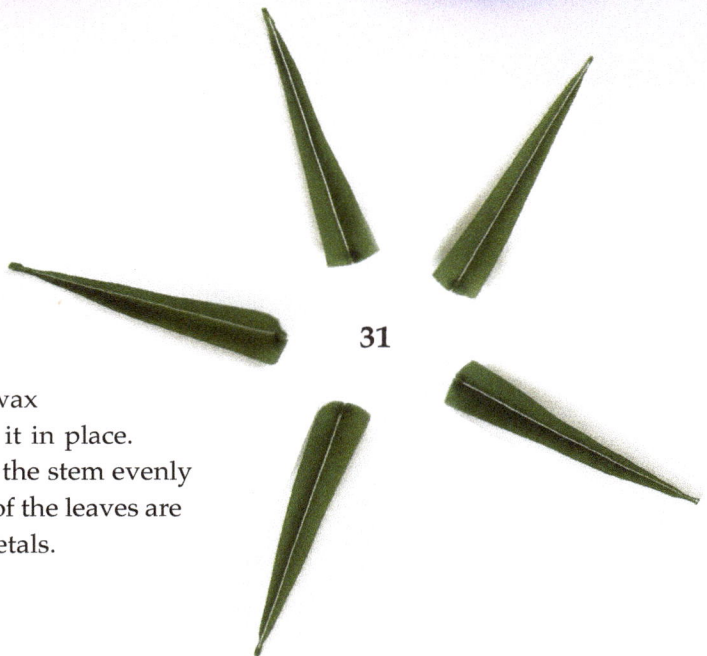

31

You will now need a sheath made from very pale wax. Using a spoon as before, make one piece taken from the back of the spoon. Trim it so that the top is pointed, them attach it round the petals, leaves and stem, pressing the base firmly into place. (Picture 32)

Your crocus is now complete. I filled a pot with dry oasis and spread glue on the surface and coated it with compost. Why dry, pour off any surplus compost. You can then push the stems of three crocuses into place. (Picture 33)

32

33

Other flowers

Up to now we have only made flowers on stems, but if you want to make a water lily, although it has a stem, you don't see it because it is underwater. You make the petals on spoons as for the crocus, again choosing a spoon as near as the shape you want. I use a teaspoon and a dessert spoon in Viners Shape (see picture of spoons – left hand two). Make eight large and eight small petals. You will use the petal on the inside of the bowl of the spoon for these. I have used pink wax.

You will need to make a wax base to attach the petals to. I use an aluminium tube, but a piece of wooden dowel about 30mm diameter will do equally well. If you are using a tube, dip it into the water and washing up liquid, (Picture 34) before dipping into the wax for the first time. (Picture 35) As each layer cools, repeat until you have a disc about

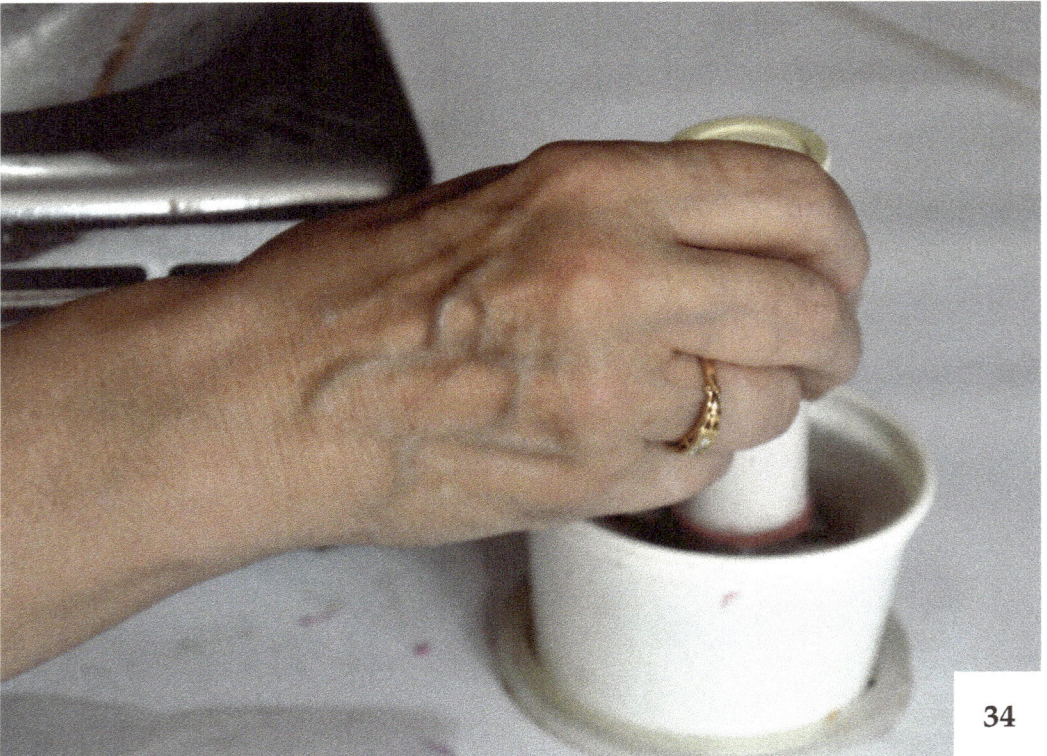

34

35

36

4mm thick. Trim any excess wax off the tube and the disc and leave to cool. If you are using wooden dowel, soak the end in water to stop the wax sticking and proceed as before.

Trim the petals into shape. (Picture 36 & 37) Then, starting with the large petals, press the base of each firmly onto the edge of the disc, forming a cross. (Picture 38) Attach the other four large petals with the base of the petal into the centre of the disc and between the first row of petals. (Picture 39) This will give the effect of a smaller petal. Now attach the first four small petals between the previous row, attaching them to where the edge of the disc is. (Picture 40) Then attach the remaining four petals, again between the previous row, but into the centre of the disc. (see pictures)

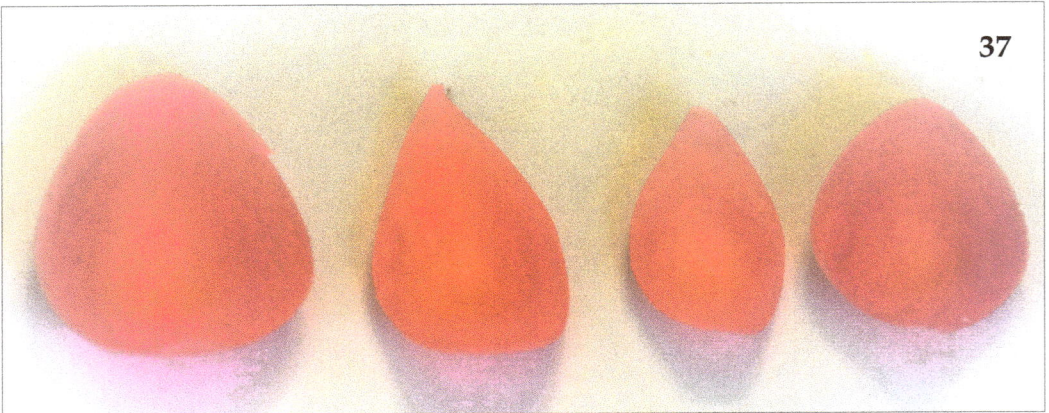

37

38

39

40

Now, with some scraps of a yellow wax sheet, roll them into a cigar shape for the centre. (Picture 41) You will need a number of stamens, made as before, about 16 if the stamens are quite thick, a lot more if you have used thinner thread. Press the stamens onto the base of the centre, so they are spaced around it. (Picture 42) Now with a pointed knife or a knitting needle, ream a hole through the centre of the disc. (Picture 43) Dip the base of the centre into molten wax and then press it firmly into the hole in the disc and leave to cool. When it has cooled, arrange the stamens into curves round the centre and then, ease the four inside petals, bending them up to the centre. Continue with all but the first row. (Picture 44) Only pick up the water lily by the centre. It is a good idea to paint melted wax onto the backs of the first row of petals to stabilise them. (Picture 45)

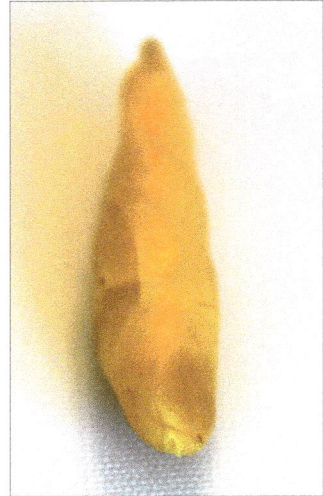

41

42

43

44

45

To make a lily pad, make a large sheet of green wax and cut out a circle. Make a slit into the centre, curving the edges upwards and sit your water lily on top. (Picture 46)

Although I have given you patterns for the roses and leaves, it is better for you to take apart a real flower, to see how nature made it and to make your own patterns from this.

46

Singapore Orchid

Foundation flowers

You can also make flowers from coloured foundation. They have the advantage of you not needing quantities of clean wax from which to make the coloured sheets, but you can shape the petals with your fingers as before. For these flowers I have used cutters made to cut petals and leaves for sugar paste flowers, (Picture 47) but you can make your own cardboard patterns if you wish.

47

For the water lily, start by cutting 5 circular discs about 30mm in diameter and pile them up to make a base. They will squash down as you add the petals. Cut 8 large and 8 small petals and shape them with your fingers so that they are cupped. Add them in the same way as for the water lily made from petal shapes on spoons. Roll some scraps of foundation to make a centre about 33mm long and cigar shaped, with a point at each end. Here, I have used bought stamens from sugar paste suppliers, but if you have your own wax, you can make your own as shown previously. Make a bundle of bought stamens, which are double ended and cut them in half. Arrange them round the centre and press them firmly into place. Attach your own stamens in the same way.

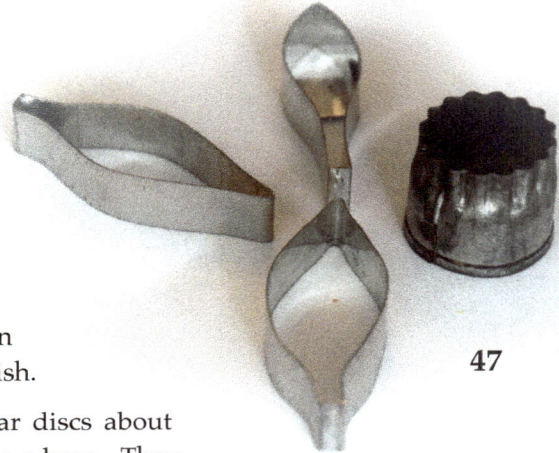

48

Melt a small amount of off cuts of wax in a bowl over water. Make a hole in the centre of the base, using a pointed knife or knitting needle. Dip the centre into the molten wax and press into the centre of the flower. Leave until cold, then arrange the stamens and ease the 3 centre rows of petals towards the centre. Cut a circle of green foundation 140mm in diameter to form the lily pad. Cut a slot into the middle of the pad and curl up all the edges. Sit your water lily on the pad. (Picture 48)

If you are feeling more adventurous, you could try a clematis. Here's one I made earlier. I really can't describe how to make it, but there are some photographs to give you an idea.

49

Attaching wires to petals with molten wax

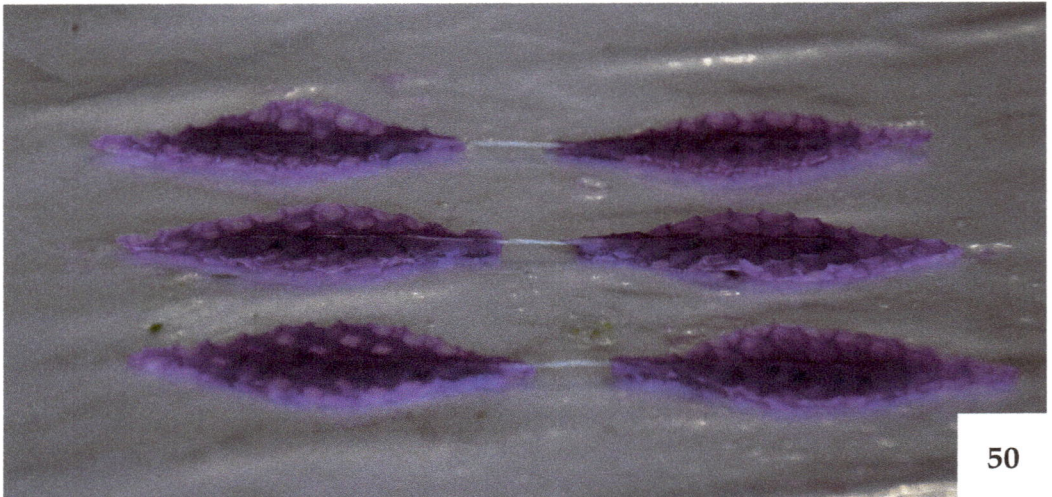

50

All six petals attached to wires

Joining petals together

Petals and stamens attached to stem

53

Join two or three leaves together

I hope I have fired your imagination to try your own wax flowers. I think I have given enough methods and materials to get you going. In this book (pages 44–46), I have included pictures of other flowers I have made, to give ideas for what can be achieved.

54

Assembled clematis

55

Aquilegias

I always try to get the wax flowers as much like the real ones as possible. With the Aquilegias, I counted the number of stamens. There were 24 thin green ones with no pollen blobs and 24 thin green ones with yellow pollen blobs, grouped round the others in the centre.

56

Rhododendron

With the Rhododendron, I didn't think a vase or plant pot would look right. I had found the piece of driftwood some time earlier and I think this looks just right.

57

Alstromerias

With the Alstromerias, I only made one stem with several flowers and buds, which works well in a bud vase.

I have been making wax flowers for a long time and I must say that I have really enjoyed it.
I hope you will too.

Elizabeth Duffin

www.ingramcontent.com/pod-product-compliance
Lightning Source LLC
LaVergne TN
LVHW070838080426
835511LV00023B/3470